EMBELLISHED MEMORIES

Embellished memories

DECORATING MATS AND FRAMES

Norma Rapko Vargas

Martingale & COMPANY

Embellished Memories:
Decorating Mats and Frames
© 2008 by Norma Rapko Vargas

If you have any questions or comments,
please contact:

Empire Road Productions
Jo Packham
215 Historic 25th Street
Ogden, Utah 84401
801-621-2777
www.empireroadproductions.com

Martingale & Company®
20205 144th Ave. NE
Woodinville, WA 98072-8478 USA
www.martingale-pub.com

Credits

President & CEO	Tom Wierzbicki
Publisher	Jane Hamada
Editorial Director	Mary V. Green
Managing Editor	Tina Cook
Designer	Matt Shay
Photographer	Zac Williams
Copy Editor	Jenn Gibbs
Assistant Copy Editor	Deborah Moeller

Printed in China
13 12 11 10 09 08   8 7 6 5 4 3 2 1

Library of Congress Cataloging-in-Publication Data is available on request.

ISBN: 978-1-56477-874-1

Mission Statement

Dedicated to providing quality products and service to inspire creativity.

DEDICATION

For Darin, Andrew, and Brooke

CONTENTS

introduction PAGE 8

chapter one VINTAGE TREASURES 14

chapter two FAMILY FAVORITES 26

chapter three CONTEMPORARY COOL 36

chapter four NATURAL INSPIRATION 44

chapter five SPECIAL OCCASIONS 52

resources PAGE **60**

acknowledgments PAGE **61**

metric conversion chart PAGE **62**

index PAGE **63**

Introduction

A child, a friend, a bride and groom, the family gathered for celebration—whatever the subject, our photographs have the power to retrieve whole scenes from our memories and to preserve them for future generations. This is why family photographs rank among our treasures, and it's why I fell in love with finding new and unusual ways to display them. A mat and frame are like the scenery for a play a photo stars in, or a costume a photo wears. The way you dress a photo can help others feel about it the way you do.

Years ago, I began to experiment with designing displays around special photos of my kids. The process was fun and, I'll admit, it felt good to have something unique to hang on the wall. Soon, friends, friends-of-friends, then perfect strangers were commissioning me to invent unusual displays for their important images, and a business was born. Years later, I'm as passionate as ever about this art form, and I'm excited to share my approach with others who want the pleasure of crafting mats and frames that are as special as the memories that inspire them.

This book is for you, whether you're an absolute beginner or a longtime crafter. The twenty-six projects here combine basic techniques from scrapbooking, altered art, faux finishing, and other crafts. Many of them can be completed in a very short time, making them ideal for crafting parties, gifting, or any time you have the urge to break out the supplies and get creative, and the designs are easy to personalize further if you substitute the suggested embellishments with pieces that have special meaning to you. As you'll see, it can be surprisingly easy to create sophisticated, original displays that fit your photos perfectly.

Sweet Remembrance.

In the Studio

As with most designers, I draw inspiration for my projects from many things. To make sure I don't miss an idea that could turn into a design, I keep a sketchbook on me and take a little time each day to use it. It also helps to have a designated work space. Not only is it convenient to have my supplies handy when the mood to create strikes, but just being in my space can get me thinking. These days, my work space is a fully stocked studio, but I used to work at the kitchen table. If you're interested in developing your own signature style for embellished mats and frames, you can use your work space and journal to explore various sources of inspiration.

Other People

I love to learn from the best! Since you're holding this book, you probably don't need me to tell you that learning how others put together their creations can help you see more possibilities for your own projects. Reading, taking a class, and looking closely at the mats and frames you see in shops can really boost your creativity.

Personal History

A lot of my inspiration comes from the time I spent as a kid in my family's clothing factory and my dad's carpentry shop. I often use fabrics in my projects and, like my dad, I'm comfortable using hardware and adapting materials to suit my vision. Think about what unique combination of skills and influences you bring to the table: they may hold the key to your personal style.

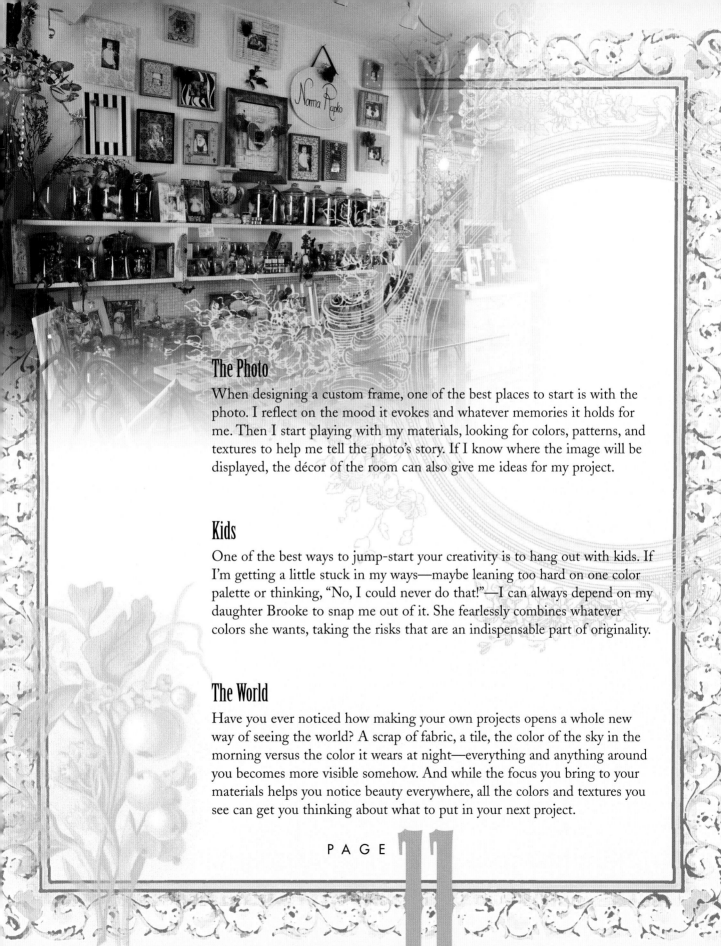

The Photo

When designing a custom frame, one of the best places to start is with the photo. I reflect on the mood it evokes and whatever memories it holds for me. Then I start playing with my materials, looking for colors, patterns, and textures to help me tell the photo's story. If I know where the image will be displayed, the décor of the room can also give me ideas for my project.

Kids

One of the best ways to jump-start your creativity is to hang out with kids. If I'm getting a little stuck in my ways—maybe leaning too hard on one color palette or thinking, "No, I could never do that!"—I can always depend on my daughter Brooke to snap me out of it. She fearlessly combines whatever colors she wants, taking the risks that are an indispensable part of originality.

The World

Have you ever noticed how making your own projects opens a whole new way of seeing the world? A scrap of fabric, a tile, the color of the sky in the morning versus the color it wears at night—everything and anything around you becomes more visible somehow. And while the focus you bring to your materials helps you notice beauty everywhere, all the colors and textures you see can get you thinking about what to put in your next project.

Background Materials

Each of the projects in this book uses one or more of the following materials as the basis for the mat or frame. If you don't have the exact background item listed in a project's instructions, consider substituting a different one and adapting the design accordingly. The key to framing memories, I find, is to have fun and be flexible. After all, it's through variations and experimentation that you'll create the most original displays.

Precut Mat Boards

While you can certainly cut your own mats, precut mat boards can be well worth the expense. They offer professional-looking results and save time better spent on more fun, creative aspects of a project.

Stretched Artist Canvases

Traditionally, artists purchased canvas cut from a roll that they then tacked onto wooden frames they built themselves and covered with gesso, a special kind of primer. Thankfully, we only have to head to the craft or art supply store to pick up canvases that are already stretched onto frames and primed, making them project-ready.

Foam-Core Board/Recycled Cardboard

Foam-core board is a lightweight, versatile material that's easy to cut and work with. I often use it to add dimension to my mats and frames. You can substitute corrugated cardboard—just give it a coat or two of gesso if the dark color will interfere with your project.

Ready-Made Frames

I often look for a solid wood frame that has lots of surface to play with, but virtually any frame can become part of a project. The three-dimensional profile of embellishments often calls for leaving the glass off the final piece (I do this so often, I created a project just to use my extra glass—it's on page 44). Sometimes, I'll use a frame that's gorgeous as-is to add another layer of beauty to a project without adding more time.

chapter one

VINTAGE TREASURES

L'amour Toujours

Materials

- Bright blue "L'amour Toujours" printed ribbon
- Button
- Gold acrylic paint
- Hot glue gun and glue sticks
- Matte decoupage glue
- "Memories" mini-frame embellishment
- Patterned papers (cream, tan, yellow)
- Photo
- Photo mounts
- Pine wood plaque
- Scissors
- Silk velvet flower
- Sponge brushes (2)

METHOD

1. Cut the cream patterned paper to cover the front of the plaque. Cut one strip each of the yellow and the tan patterned papers long enough to cover the width of the plaque. Cut the ribbon to the width of the plaque. Set the papers and ribbon aside.

2. Using a sponge brush, paint the edges of the plaque gold; let dry

3. With a different sponge brush, apply a light coat of decoupage glue to the front of the plaque. Place the cream patterned paper on the wet glue and gently smooth out any wrinkles. Repeat to apply the yellow and the tan strips of paper.

4. Apply a light coat of decoupage glue to seal the paper. While the decoupage glue is still wet, apply the ribbon.

5. When the surface of the plaque is dry, apply photo mounts to the back of the photo and adhere the photo to the plaque.

6. Hot glue the silk velvet flower and button to the top left corner of the photo and the "Memories" mini-frame embellishment below the photo.

VINTAGE BLISS

Materials

- Black ribbon
- Clear plastic picture frame
- Cream-and-tan text collage patterned paper
- Fabric rose garland
- Hot glue gun and glue sticks
- Photo
- Rhinestone shoe buckle
- Ruler
- Scissors
- Small screw-in eyehooks (2)
- Spray adhesive
- Stretched artist canvas
- Taupe raw silk fabric

METHOD

1. Cut your fabric to cover the front and sides of the canvas. Spray the back of the fabric with spray adhesive, wait a moment, and apply the fabric to the canvas.

2. Cut the paper 1" smaller than the canvas. Spray the back of the paper with spray adhesive and place the paper right side up on the fabric.

3. Hot glue the picture frame to the center of the embellished canvas. With small beads of hot glue, add ribbon along the edge of the frame.

4. Screw the eyehooks into the back of the canvas, 1" down from each top corner. Thread each end of the fabric rose garland through an eyehook and twist or knot it to secure.

5. Thread the ribbon through the rhinestone shoe buckle. Hot glue the buckle and ribbon to the center of the garland.

6. Insert the photo into the plastic frame.

Milagros

Materials

- Angel embellishment
- Assorted crosses (5)
- Brown antiquing medium
- Craft glue
- Cream dimensional paint
- Gold metal scroll appliqué
- Gold metallic marker
- Hot glue gun and glue sticks
- Loose crystals
- Madonna medallion
- Matte decoupage glue
- Newspaper
- Palette knife
- Photo
- Rag
- Rhinestone chain
- Sponge brush
- Stretched artist canvas
- Tweezers

METHOD

1. Spread newspaper to protect your work surface. Place the canvas on it, right side up, and squeeze a wavy line of the dimensional paint onto the canvas. Using a palette knife, gently spread the paint, creating a heavily textured surface. Allow the paint to dry completely.

2. Using a rag, apply antiquing medium to the dried dimensional paint. Rub off the excess antiquing medium.

3. Use a sponge brush to apply a light coat of decoupage glue to the back of the photo. Place the photo on the canvas and gently smooth out any wrinkles.

4. Seal the photo with a light coat of decoupage glue.

5. Using the gold metallic marker, line the edges of the photo and canvas.

6. Hot glue the metal scroll appliqué to the top of the canvas, and then glue one cross onto the front of the scroll. Hot glue the Madonna medallion onto the front of the cross. (The three items will be layered when you're done.) Hot glue the rhinestone chain to the edge of the Madonna medallion; trim off extra.

7. Hot glue one cross to each corner of the frame and the angel embellishment to the bottom center.

8. Apply a loose crystal to the center of each cross using tweezers and craft glue.

La Niña Bella

Materials

- 2"-wide masking tape
- Acrylic paint (light turquoise, pink)
- Chipboard glitter piece
- Craft glue
- Hot glue gun and glue sticks
- Loose crystals
- Matte decoupage glue
- Metal bird
- Photo
- Scissors
- Silk flowers
- Small glass bottle
- Sponge brushes (3)
- Spray of velvet leaves
- Stretched artist canvas
- Tweezers
- Vintage-style flower brooch

METHOD

1. Using a sponge brush, paint the canvas pink. Allow it to dry.

2. To create the stripes, use masking tape to block off the areas that will remain pink, making the space for the center blue stripe wider than the others. With a different sponge brush, paint the exposed areas light turquoise.

3. Cut your photo into an oval shape. With a third sponge brush, apply a light coat of decoupage glue to the back of the photo. Place the photo on the canvas and gently smooth out any wrinkles.

4. Seal the photo with another light coat of decoupage glue.

5. Apply loose crystals along the left half of the oval photo using tweezers and craft glue.

6. Hot glue silk flowers, the spray of velvet leaves, and other embellishments along the right side of the photo, leaving a small gap for the brooch just under the velvet leaves. Pin the brooch to a leaf, allowing it to be removable and wearable.

Marie Antoinette

Materials

Acrylic paint (iridescent gold, teal)

Assorted fabric leaves and flowers

Cardboard

Craft glue

Foam dots

Hot glue gun and glue sticks

Image of Marie Antoinette
(about half the size of the frame opening)

Loose crystals

Marker

Matte decoupage glue

Metal butterflies

Metal rose

Nameplate

Patterned papers (cream text, yellow)

Pink-and-white striped text cardstock

Pink metal lace corners

Scissors (plain, scalloped)

Small tin bowl

Sponge brushes (3)

Tweezers

Unfinished wood frame

METHOD

1. Remove the glass from the frame and save it for another project. Using a sponge brush, paint the frame teal. Allow it to dry completely.

2. With a different sponge brush, paint gold stripes freehand. Allow the paint to dry completely.

3. Apply loose crystals to the inside border of the frame using tweezers and craft glue.

4. Hot glue the fabric leaves and flowers and the metal rose to the top left corner of the frame, and the butterflies and small tin bowl along the bottom right side. Hot glue the metal lace corners to the frame.

5. Cut a small piece of yellow patterned paper to fit the nameplate. Write a message on it using the marker, slip it into the nameplate, and hot glue the nameplate to the bottom of the frame.

6. Cut a piece of cardboard to fit into the frame. Use a third sponge brush to apply a light coat of decoupage glue to the cardboard. Place cream text patterned paper on the cardboard and gently smooth out any wrinkles. Allow the glue to dry.

7. Using scalloped scissors, cut the cardstock about ½" smaller on all sides than the cardboard. Use the craft glue to adhere the image of Marie Antoinette to the cardstock, and then use foam dots to apply the cardstock to the cardboard.

8. Insert the project into the frame.

Pretty Little Plate

Materials

Blue ribbon bow

Crystal button

Embossed metal crown

Hot glue gun and glue sticks

Metal wreath embellishment

Photo

Photo mounts

Ruler

Scissors

Small plate

METHOD

1. Using your plate as a template, measure and cut the photo to fit the center of the plate.

2. Apply photo mounts to the back of the photo and adhere the photo to the center of the plate.

3. Hot glue the metal wreath embellishment over the photo, the ribbon bow to the top of the wreath, and the crystal button to the center of the bow. Hot glue the embossed metal crown to the top back of the plate.

Something Blue

Materials

- Acrylic paint (gold, light blue)
- Brown antiquing medium
- Gold photo corners
- Hot glue gun and glue sticks
- Photo
- Photo mounts
- Rag
- Sponge brushes (2)
- Stretched artist canvas
- Wood scroll appliqué

METHOD

1. Using a sponge brush, paint the canvas and scroll appliqué blue. Before the paint dries completely, add swipes of gold paint with a different sponge brush.

2. Using a rag, wipe off some of the gold paint, leaving only highlights. Allow it to dry.

3. With the same rag, wipe brown antiquing medium on the canvas. Allow it to dry.

4. Hot glue the appliqué to the top of the canvas. Apply photo mounts to the back of the photo and adhere the photo to the canvas. Apply the photo corners to all four corners.

FAIRYTALE DREAMS

Materials

- Chipboard letters
- Craft glue
- Craft knife
- Fabric flower
- Hot glue gun and glue sticks
- Lilac raw silk fabric
- Loose crystals
- Photo
- Precut mat board
- Ruler
- Scissors
- Spray adhesive
- Tweezers
- Vintage-style brooch
- White frame

METHOD

1. Cut your fabric to the dimensions of the mat plus 1" on all sides (including the inner window).

2. Spray your mat board with spray adhesive. Wait a few seconds, and then place your fabric on the glue. Gently smooth out any wrinkles.

3. Using a craft knife, cut each inner corner at a 45-degree angle. Spray the back of the overhanging fabric with spray adhesive, and then fold it around to the back of the mat and smooth it into place. Trim any excess fabric along the outer edges so that it is flush with the mat.

4. Hot glue a fabric flower and the brooch to the top left corner of the window. Arrange chipboard letters along the bottom of the mat and hot glue them into place.

5. Apply loose crystals to the chipboard letters using tweezers and craft glue. Allow the glue to dry thoroughly.

6. Insert the photo and mat into the frame. If you have difficulty inserting the embellished mat into the frame, remove the glass from the frame and save it for another project.

BROOKE

Briar Rose

Materials

Antiqued green frame

Brown antiquing medium

Hot glue gun and glue sticks

Metal leaves

Metal roses

Photo

Precut mat board

Spray paint for metal
(burnt red, green)

METHOD

1. Spray paint the metal roses with the burnt red spray paint.

2. Spray paint the metal leaves with the green spray paint.

3. When the leaves are dry, use your finger to rub a small amount of brown antiquing medium on them.

4. Hot glue the leaves and roses to the top and bottom of the mat. Allow the glue to harden thoroughly.

5. Remove the glass from the frame and save it for another project. Insert the photo and mat into the frame.

PRINCESS ALBUM

Materials

Assorted type letters

Blue crystal-beaded chain

Craft glue

Fabric-covered photo album with a front window

Gold metal lace corners (4)

Grommets and small hammer

Hot glue gun and glue sticks

Hot pink ribbon

Loose crystals

Metal leaves

Metal rose

Photo

Small metal flowers

Spray paint for metal (burnt umber, green)

Tweezers

METHOD

1. Spray the metal rose and small metal flowers with burnt umber paint and spray the metal leaves with green paint. Allow them to dry completely.

2. Hot glue the leaves, rose, and small flowers to the cover of the photo album, above and below the window.

3. Hot glue the metal lace corners to the album cover and the assorted type letters to the bottom of the cover.

4. Apply loose crystals along the window in the album cover using tweezers and craft glue. Place a grommet over each crystal and lightly hammer into place.

5. Place the ribbon on the inside of the album's front cover and the crystal-beaded chain along the outside of the album's spine. Tie the ribbon to the chain at the top and bottom of the spine to secure.

6. Insert the photo into the window of the album cover.

Mon Amie

Materials

- Blue velvet ribbon
- Buttons (2)
- Craft glue
- Craft knife
- Gold metal lace corners (2)
- Hot glue gun and glue sticks
- Loose crystals
- Matte decoupage glue
- Patterned papers (blue scroll, pink patchwork)
- Photo
- Pink "Mon amie" printed ribbon
- Scissors
- Sponge brush
- Tweezers
- Unfinished pine frame

METHOD

1. Using a sponge brush, apply a light coat of decoupage glue to the top half of the frame. Lay the blue scroll patterned paper over the wet glue and gently smooth out any wrinkles.

2. Repeat step 1 with the pink patchwork patterned paper, but adhere it to the bottom half of the frame only.

3. Using a craft knife, cut out the paper at the center of the frame.

4. Apply a light coat of decoupage glue to seal the paper.

5. Cut two pieces of "Mon amie" printed ribbon to go across the sides of the frame. Hot glue them into place. Repeat with the blue velvet ribbon, and then hot glue a button to the center of each velvet ribbon.

6. Hot glue the metal lace corners to the top of the frame.

7. Apply loose crystals to the pink patchwork patterned paper, using tweezers and craft glue. Allow the glue to dry thoroughly.

8. Insert the photo into the frame.

Dear Mommy

Materials

- 24-gauge wire
- Blue crystal-beaded chain
- Craft glue
- Craft knife
- Cream patterned paper
- Glitter
- Gold metal lace corners (2)
- Handwritten note
- Hot glue gun and glue sticks
- Matte decoupage glue
- Photo
- Plastic frame
- Ruler
- Scissors
- Screw-in eyehooks (2)
- Silk roses with wire stems
- Sponge brush
- Stretched artist canvas
- Wire cutters

METHOD

1. Using a sponge brush, apply a light coat of decoupage glue to the canvas. Lay the paper over the wet glue and gently smooth out any wrinkles. Use a craft knife to trim any excess paper.

2. Insert the photo into the plastic frame. Hot glue the plastic frame to the top of the canvas and the metal lace corners to opposite corners of the frame.

3. Cut the handwritten note into a heart shape, apply craft glue to its borders, and sprinkle the note with glitter. Allow the note to dry, and then hot glue it to the canvas.

4. Screw the eyehooks into the top corners of the canvas. To secure the crystal-beaded chain to the canvas, cut a 3" length of wire and thread it through one end of the chain and an eyehook. Twist the ends of the wire several times to secure it. Repeat on the other side.

5. Twist the wire stems of the silk roses around the left side of the crystal-beaded chain.

chapter three

CONTEMPORARY COOL

Glitzy Glass

Materials

Gloves

Hot glue gun and glue sticks

Newspaper

Photo

Photo-safe tape

Precut mat board

Reddish brown ribbon bow

Reddish brown, tumbled, cut glass

Safety glasses

METHOD

1. Put on gloves and safety glasses to prepare yourself for handling glass. (Note: Though your tumbled glass pieces should be relatively smooth, it's always good to put safety first!)

2. Cover part of the mat board with a thick coat of hot glue. Apply a handful of glass to the glue and gently pat it into the glue.

3. When the glue has hardened, gently brush or shake off the excess glass onto the newspaper.

4. Repeat steps 2 and 3 until the entire mat board is covered.

5. Hot glue the ribbon bow to the back of the mat board so that the bow is visible from the front.

6. Place the window of the mat over the photo and secure the photo with tape.

COUNTRY HEART

Materials

- 24-gauge wire
- Gold metal lace corners (4)
- Hot glue gun and glue sticks
- Paper piercer
- Photo
- Photo-safe tape
- Precut foam-core mat
- Sage green acrylic paint
- Sponge brush
- Wire cutters

METHOD

1. Using a sponge brush, paint the mat sage green.

2. Use wire cutters to cut a length of 24-gauge wire about eight times as long as your mat is tall. Bend the wire in half and twist the two halves together. Bend the twisted wire in half and use the wire cutters to squeeze the center tight.

3. Bend the two halves of the twisted wire to form a heart shape, wrapping one end around the other to create a long point at the bottom of the heart.

4. Trim the ends of the wire with the wire cutters.

5. Place the heart on the mat and, using the paper piercer, punch two small holes on either side of the heart's top left half and two small holes on the heart's top right half.

6. Cut a short length of 24-gauge wire. With the front of the mat facing you, thread the short wire through one of the holes from the back to the front. Bend the short wire around one side of the wire heart and through the other hole. Twist together the two ends of the short wire, securing one side of the heart to the mat. Repeat to secure the other side of the heart.

7. Hot glue the metal lace corners to the mat.

8. Place the window of the mat over the photo and secure the photo with tape.

Precious Little One

Materials

- 3" lengths of 24-gauge wire (2)
- Amber crystal beaded chain
- Antiqued gold metal lace corners (2)
- Blue ribbon
- Bubble sticker
- Craft glue
- Craft knife
- Craft stick
- Cream-and-gold patterned paper
- Fabric flower
- Fabric leaf
- Foam-core board
- Hot glue gun and glue sticks
- Large picture frame
- Loose crystals
- Pen (optional)
- Photo
- Picture-mounting glue
- Rub-on phrase or letters and craft stick
- Ruler
- Scissors
- Screw-in eyehooks (2)
- Small oval frame
- Small piece of paper
- Spray adhesive
- Tarnished brass metal frame corners (4)
- Taupe raw silk fabric
- Tiny metal frame
- Tweezers
- Type letters (L, O, V, E)
- Vintage-style brooch
- Wire cutters

METHOD

1. Using a craft knife, cut the foam-core board to fit inside the large picture frame. Using scissors, cut the fabric to cover the board.

2. Spray the board with spray adhesive. Wait a few moments, and then place your fabric right side up on the glue. Gently smooth out any wrinkles.

3. Cut your patterned paper 1½" smaller than the board on all sides. Spray the back of the paper with spray adhesive and apply the paper to the board.

4. Position your rub-on phrase or letters on the bottom left corner of the paper and use the craft stick to apply.

5. Using picture-mounting glue, apply your photo to the center of the board.

6. Hot glue the small oval frame to the board, over the photo; the metal lace corners to two opposite corners of the paper; and the type letters to the right side of the paper.

7. Place the board inside the large frame and secure it with the frame backing. Hot glue the metal frame corners to the frame.

8. Screw the eyehooks into the top corners of the large frame. Wrap one 3" length of 24-gauge wire through one end of the crystal chain and an eyehook. Twist it several times to secure and trim any excess wire. Repeat on the other side.

9. Hot glue the fabric flower and leaf and the vintage-style brooch to the top left corner of the frame.

10. Apply rub-on letters or write the words "Precious Little One" on the small piece of paper. Slip the paper into the tiny frame and apply the bubble sticker over the words. Thread blue ribbon through the loop at the top of the tiny frame and hot glue the ends of the ribbon to the metal rose. Note: If your tiny frame does not have a loop, hot glue the ribbon to the back of the frame.

11. Apply loose crystals to the small oval frame using the tweezers and craft glue.

COWBOY

Materials

24-gauge wire	Tacks and a hammer
Needle-nose pliers	Unfinished wood frame
Photo	White acrylic paint
Sandpaper	Wire cutters
Sponge brush	

METHOD

1. Using a sponge brush, apply a light coat of white paint to the frame. Allow it to dry completely.

2. Lightly sand the entire frame, removing some of the paint from the edges.

3. Hammer the tacks at regular intervals around the center of the frame.

4. Cut a long piece of 24-gauge wire. Using needle-nose pliers and your fingers, shape the word "Cowboy."

5. Attach the wire word to the frame with a few more tacks. (Place the tacks where you've overlapped the wire to help secure the letter shapes.)

6. Insert the photo into the frame.

Starfish

Materials

- Bird rubber stamp
- Craft glue
- Fabric leaf
- Glass
- Glitter
- Gold dusting powder
- Gold metal lace corners (2)
- Hot glue gun and glue sticks
- Photo and photo mounts
- Rubber-stamping medium
- Scissors
- Shallow dish for glue
- Silver duct tape
- Silver metal ball chain
- Small brush
- Small crown
- Starfish

METHOD

1. Cut a strip of duct tape as long as one side of the glass, and then cut it in half lengthwise to create two thin strips of tape. Apply one strip to one edge of the glass, wrapping it around the front and back, and apply the other strip to the opposite edge of the glass.

2. Repeat step 1 to cover the remaining two edges of the glass.

3. Hot glue the metal lace corners to opposite corners of the glass, and then hot glue the ends of the metal ball chain to the top back edge of the glass.

4. Pour craft glue into a shallow dish. Dip the starfish in the glue and sprinkle it with glitter.

5. Hot glue the starfish, crown, and fabric leaf to the top left corner of the glass.

6. Load the rubber stamp with stamping medium and stamp the glass. Before it sets, use the small brush to dust it with gold powder.

7. Use photo mounts to apply your photo to either the front of the glass (plaque-style) or to the back (traditional frame style) as you prefer.

Seaside

Materials

- Acrylic paint (black, brown, dark blue)
- Double-layered, ivory, precut mat board
- Gold metal lace corners (4)
- Hot glue gun and glue sticks
- Key
- Metal crown embellishment
- Metal wreath embellishment
- Nail-head ribbon
- Photo
- Seashell
- Sponge brushes (3)
- Spray of pearls
- Starfish
- String
- Unfinished pine wood frame
- Wire cutters

METHOD

1. Using a sponge brush, paint the frame brown. Set it aside to dry.

2. Using a different sponge brush, paint the outer layer of the mat black. Allow it to dry, and then use another sponge brush to add highlights with blue paint. (The inside edge of the window should remain the original color of the mat.)

3. Cut a length of nail-head ribbon for each side of the mat window and hot glue each one into place.

4. Hot glue metal lace corners to the frame.

5. Tie the string to the key and hot glue it to the top left corner of the frame along with the seashell, spray of pearls, crown, and wreath. Hot glue the starfish to the bottom right corner of the frame.

6. Remove the glass from the frame and save it for another project. Insert the photo and the mat into the frame.

SONG BIRD

Materials

- Brown ribbon
- Craft knife
- Hot glue gun and glue sticks
- Matte decoupage glue
- Metal butterfly embellishment
- Needle-nose pliers
- Patterned papers (birds, sheet music)
- Photo
- Pine wood plaque
- Plastic frame
- Scissors
- Spanish moss
- Sponge brush
- Square metal embellishment

METHOD

1. Using a sponge brush, apply a light coat of decoupage glue to the plaque. Lay the sheet music patterned paper over the wet glue and gently smooth out any wrinkles. Use a craft knife to trim any excess paper.

2. Cut a strip of the birds patterned paper to cover the bottom of the frame. Apply a light coat of decoupage glue to the back of the paper strip and adhere it to the plaque. Gently smooth out any wrinkles.

3. Apply a small line of decoupage glue across the plaque and adhere the ribbon over the seam between the two patterns of paper.

4. Using needle-nose pliers, bend the square metal embellishment into a flat-bottomed "U" shape. Position the plastic frame on the plaque to locate the center point just below the frame. Set the frame aside and hot glue the bent metal embellishment to the center point. (The bottom of the frame will rest inside it.)

5. Insert the photo into the plastic frame and hot glue Spanish moss around the edges of the frame.

6. Hot glue the plastic frame to the wood plaque, resting the bottom of the frame in the bent metal embellishment.

7. Hot glue the butterfly to the moss at the top right corner of the frame.

Sweet Remembrance.

Leopard King

Materials

Beaded bracelet or miniature rosary (optional)

Craft glue

Craft knife

Embossed metal crown

Gold acrylic paint

Hot glue gun and glue sticks

Leopard-print patterned paper

Loose crystals

Matte decoupage glue

Photo

Precut mat board

Scissors

Sponge brushes (2)

Tweezers

Unfinished wood frame

METHOD

1. Using a sponge brush, paint the frame gold. Allow the paint to dry completely.

2. Cut the paper to cover the mat. Leave the center intact (you will cut it out later).

3. Using a different sponge brush, apply a light coat of decoupage glue to the mat. Lay the paper over the wet glue and gently smooth out any wrinkles.

4. Using a craft knife, cut out the paper around the center of the mat.

5. Apply a light coat of decoupage glue to seal the paper. Allow it to dry.

6. Insert the photo, mat, and glass into the frame.

7. Hot glue the embossed metal crown to the top center of the frame or, if you prefer, directly onto the glass. (The photo shows each option.)

8. Apply the loose crystals to the crown using tweezers and craft glue. If desired, dangle a favorite memento such as a beaded bracelet or miniature rosary over one corner of the frame.

THE GLOBE
ILLUSTRATED
SHAKESPEARE

THE COMPLETE WORKS
ANNOTATED

HEUREUX ANNIVERSAIRE

Materials

"Heureux Anniversaire" rubber stamp

Black spray paint

Black stamp ink

Brown antiquing medium

Cream acrylic paint

French button beads

Gold metal lace corners (2)

Hot glue gun and glue sticks

Large scroll embellishments (2)

Matte decoupage glue

Photo

Rag

Red ribbon

Scissors

Sponge brushes (2)

Stretched artist canvas

METHOD

1. Using a sponge brush, paint the canvas cream. Allow it to dry.

2. Use a rag to rub antiquing medium over the canvas.

3. Spray paint the scroll embellishments black. Set them aside to dry.

4. Cut the photo into a circle. Using a different sponge brush, apply a light coat of decoupage glue to the back of the photo. Place the photo on the canvas and gently smooth out any wrinkles.

5. Hot glue the metal lace corners to the top and bottom of the canvas (right side only).

6. Hot glue the French button beads around the picture.

7. Hot glue the scroll embellishments above and below the photo.

8. Use the rubber stamp and stamp ink to apply the words "Heureux Anniversaire" to the bottom of the canvas.

9. Tie the ribbon around the left side of the canvas, positioning the bow near the bottom.

Cherubs Divine Ornament

Materials

- 24-gauge wire
- Chandelier crystal
- Cherubs embellishment
- Craft knife
- Cream patterned paper
- Glass beads
- Golden brown ribbon
- Hot glue gun and glue sticks
- Matte decoupage glue
- Oval piece of cardboard
- Paper piercer
- Photo
- Photo mounts
- Sponge brush
- Wire cutters

METHOD

1. Using a sponge brush, apply a light coat of decoupage glue to the cardboard. Lay the paper over the wet glue and gently smooth out any wrinkles. Use a craft knife to trim any excess paper.

2. Apply a light coat of decoupage glue to seal the paper.

3. Add a bead of hot glue along the right side, and then pour the glass beads over the hot glue, gently pressing down on the beads. Repeat this step on the left side.

4. Hot glue the cherubs embellishment to the top.

5. Hot glue the ends of the ribbon to the back of the cardboard, near the top.

6. Apply photo mounts to the back of the photo and adhere the photo to the background.

7. Using a paper piercer, punch a small hole at the bottom of the background. Cut a short length of 24-gauge wire, thread it through the chandelier crystal and the hole you punched, and twist the ends together to secure.

N. E. ALLEN,

Artistic Photographer,

LESLIE,

MICH.

Merry Christmas

Materials

Acrylic paint (brown, pale green)

Bead board cut to fit the frame

Brown antiquing medium

Christmas-themed image

Craft glue

Glitter "Noel" chipboard embellishment

Hot glue gun and glue sticks

Matte decoupage glue

Rag

Sandpaper

Sponge brushes (3)

Wooden frame

METHOD

1. Using a sponge brush, paint the bead board pale green. Using a different sponge brush, paint the wooden frame brown. Allow them to dry.

2. Using a rag, rub the bead board and the frame with brown antiquing medium. Rub off any excess. Allow them to dry.

3. Lightly rub random spots of the frame with sandpaper to give it a distressed look.

4. Using a different sponge brush, apply a light coat of decoupage glue to the painted bead board. Lay the Christmas-themed image over the wet glue and gently smooth out any wrinkles. Apply a light coat of decoupage glue over the image to seal it. Allow it to dry.

5. Hot glue the frame to the bead board.

6. Using craft glue, adhere the "Noel" chipboard embellishment to the upper left side of the frame.

Merry Christmas

Noël

EMENTS

DÉCORATIONS

les maîtres

par

UÈGNOT

FLEUR-DE-LIS

Materials

Craft glue

Fleur-de-lis embellishment

Gold metallic marker

Hot glue gun and glue sticks

Loose crystals

Photo

Red acrylic paint

Sponge brush

Tweezers

Unfinished wood frame

METHOD

1. Using a sponge brush, apply two coats of red paint to the frame. Allow it to dry.

2. Hot glue the fleur-de-lis embellishment to the top center of the frame.

3. Apply loose crystals at regular intervals along the outer edges of the frame using tweezers and craft glue.

4. Using the gold metallic marker, draw a line along all four edges.

5. Insert the photo into the frame.

The Love Letter

Materials

- Black frame
- Craft knife
- Cream text patterned paper
- Matte decoupage glue
- Photo
- Precut mat board with beaded window
- Sponge brush

METHOD

1. Using a sponge brush, apply a light coat of decoupage glue to the mat. Lay the paper over the wet glue and gently smooth out any wrinkles.

2. Using a craft knife, trim the excess paper from the outer edges and cut out the center window.

3. Apply a light coat of decoupage glue to seal the paper.

4. Insert the photo and the mat into the frame.

PER SOLEM PINGO

V. MANDERS
The Studio
HOE STREET
WALTHAMSTOW

Resources

The examples in this book were created with materials from the following companies. While most products can be found at your local arts and crafts store, please visit my website www.normarapkovargas.com for more information on hard-to-find items.

Frames and Plaques
Walnut Hollow
www.walnuthollow.com
800-950-5101

Paints and Adhesives
Golden Artist Colors, Inc.
www.goldenpaints.com

Plaid
www.plaidonline.com
800-842-4197

Specialty Papers
Cavallini Papers & Co., Inc.
www.cavallini.com

K & Company
www.kandcompany.com
888-244-2083

Embellishments
7gypsies
www.sevengypsies.com
877-7gypsy7
877-749-7797

Art Institute Glitter, Inc.
www.artglitter.com
877-909-0805

Berwick Offray, LLC
www.offray.com

Lina G
All the Trimmings
805-772-7759

Midori, Inc.
www.midoriribbon.com
800-659-3049

Tinsel Trading Company
www.tinseltrading.com

Stamping Supplies
Ranger Industries, Inc.
www.rangerink.com
732-389-3535

Tumbled Glass
Mosaic Tile Arts
www.mosaictilearts.com

Photographs
Sharon Forbes
www.sharonforbes.com

ACKNOWLEDGMENTS

Thank you, God. Thank you, Jo Packham, for your incredible talent and guidance. You are amazing! Thank you to Jenn Gibbs, Deb Moeller, Matt Shay, and Zac Williams for your talent and vision. Thank you also to Martingale & Company—this project would not have been possible without you!

To my husband, Darin, and my loving children, Andrew and Brooke Rapko—thank you for all your love and support.

To my parents, Samuel and Amalia Vargas Garcias—por ser los mejores padres y por todo su amor!

To my siblings who feel my every emotion—Alma, Jaime, Ricardo, Samuel Vargas. I love you dearly.

Jasmine Vargas—thank you for all the love and support.

Gracias a mi mama Lupe y papa Rogelio Vargas por todo su amor y cariño y por esos días que pasamos juntos en la fábrica!

To all of my friends and family who believed in me—Robert, Lori, Christian and Hans Blanchard; Stacey Dietz, Niema Madden, Silvia and Theressa Giammarco, Kym Hoban, Cindy Vargas, Diane Fish, Kelly Stevens, and Sharon Forbes; the Herrera Family, the Vargas Family, and the Chavez Family. And last, but not least, my extended family at Northpark Community Church. I could not have done it without you!

METRIC CONVERSION CHARTS

inches	mm	cm	inches	cm	inches	cm
⅛	3	0.3	9	22.9	30	76.2
¼	6	0.6	10	25.4	31	78.7
⅜	9	0.9	11	27.9	32	81.3
½	13	1.3	12	30.5	33	83.8
⅝	16	1.6	13	33.0	34	86.4
¾	19	1.9	14	35.6	35	88.9
⅞	22	2.2	15	38.1	36	91.4
1	25	2.5	16	40.6	37	94.0
1¼	32	3.2	17	43.2	38	96.5
1½	38	3.8	18	45.7	39	99.1
1¾	44	4.4	19	48.3	40	101.6
2	51	5.1	20	50.8	41	104.1
2½	64	6.4	21	53.3	42	106.7
3	76	7.6	22	55.9	43	109.2
3½	89	8.9	23	58.4	44	111.8
4	102	10.2	24	61.0	45	114.3
4½	114	11.4	25	63.5	46	116.8
5	127	12.7	26	66.0	47	119.4
6	152	15.2	27	68.6	48	121.9
7	178	17.8	28	71.1	49	124.5
8	203	20.3	29	73.7	50	127.0

yards to meters

yards	meters	yards	meters	yards	meters	yards	meters	yards	meters
⅛	0.11	2⅛	1.94	4⅛	3.77	6⅛	5.60	8⅛	7.43
¼	0.23	2¼	2.06	4¼	3.89	6¼	5.72	8¼	7.54
⅜	0.34	2⅜	2.17	4⅜	4.00	6⅜	5.83	8⅜	7.66
½	0.46	2½	2.29	4½	4.11	6½	5.94	8½	7.77
⅝	0.57	2⅝	2.40	4⅝	4.23	6⅝	6.06	8⅝	7.89
¾	0.69	2¾	2.51	4¾	4.34	6¾	6.17	8¾	8.00
⅞	0.80	2⅞	2.63	4⅞	4.46	6⅞	6.29	8⅞	8.12
1	0.91	3	2.74	5	4.57	7	6.40	9	8.23
1⅛	1.03	3⅛	2.86	5⅛	4.69	7⅛	6.52	9⅛	8.34
1¼	1.14	3¼	2.97	5¼	4.80	7¼	6.63	9¼	8.46
1⅜	1.26	3⅜	3.09	5⅜	4.91	7⅜	6.74	9⅜	8.57
1½	1.37	3½	3.20	5½	5.03	7½	6.86	9½	8.69
1⅝	1.49	3⅝	3.31	5⅝	5.14	7⅝	6.97	9⅝	8.80
1¾	1.60	3¾	3.43	5¾	5.26	7¾	7.09	9¾	8.92
1⅞	1.71	3⅞	3.54	5⅞	5.37	7⅞	7.20	9⅞	9.03
2	1.83	4	3.66	6	5.49	8	7.32	10	9.14

Index

B

background materials, 12

Briar Rose, 28-29

C

Cherubs Divine
Ornament, 54-55

Country Heart, 38-39

Cowboy, 42-43

D

Dear Mommy, 34-35

F

Fairytale Dreams, 26-27

Fleur-de-lis, 58

foam-core board, 12

G

Glitzy Glass, 36-37

H

Heureux Anniversaire, 52-53

I

inspiration, 10-11

L

L'amour Toujours, 14-15

La Niña Bella, 20-21

Leopard King, 50-51

Love Letter, The, 59

M

Marie Antoinette, 22-23

Merry Christmas, 56-57

Milagros, 18-19

Mon Amie, 32-33

P

Precious Little One, 40-41

precut mat boards, 12

Pretty Little Plate, 24

Princess Album, 30-31

R

ready-made frames, 12

recycled cardboard, 12

S

Seaside, 46-47

Something Blue, 25

Song Bird, 48-49

Starfish, 44-45

stretched artist canvases, 12

V

Vintage Bliss, 16-17

NEW AND BESTSELLING TITLES FROM

America's Best-Loved Craft & Hobby Books®
America's Best-Loved Knitting Books®

America's Best-Loved Quilt Books®

BEADING AND JEWELRY

101 Sparkling Necklaces
The Beader's Handbook
Crochet for Beaders
The Little Box of Beaded Bracelets
    and Earrings
The Little Box of Beaded Necklaces
    and Earrings

KNITTING AND CROCHET

365 Crochet Stitches a Year:
    Perpetual Calendar
365 Knitting Stitches a Year:
    Perpetual Calendar
A to Z of Crochet—*New!*
A to Z of Knitting
Amigurumi World—*New!!*
Crocheted Pursenalities
First Crochet
First Knits
Handknit Skirts
Kitty Knits—*New!*
The Knitter's Book of Finishing
    Techniques
Knitting Circles around Socks
Knitting with Gigi
The Little Box of Crocheted Throws
The Little Box of Knitted Throws
Modern Classics
Pursenalities
Sensational Knitted Socks

MEMORY CRAFTS AND SCRAPBOOKING

Art from the Heart
Scrapbooking off the Page…
    and on the Wall
Sew Sentimental

PAPER AND FIBER CRAFTS

Card Design
Creative Embellishments
It's a Wrap
Miniature Punchneedle Embroidery
Needle-Felting Magic
**Needle Felting with Cotton and
    Wool**—*New!*
A Passion for Punchneedle
Punchneedle Fun
Sculpted Threads
Stitched Collage—*New!*

QUILTING

40 Fabulous Quick-Cut Quilts
The Americana Collection
Baby Wraps—*New!*
Calendar Kids
Christmas with Artful Offerings
Cool Girls Quilt

Copy Cat Quilts—*New!*
Creating Your Perfect Quilting Space
Even More Quilts for Baby
Happy Endings, Revised Edition
It's in the Details
Let's Quilt!
The Little Box of Baby Quilts
Mosaic Picture Quilts
Nickel Quilts
Points of View
Positively Postcards
Quilter's Block-a-Day Calendar
Quilts for Baby
Quilts on the Double
Sew Fun, Sew Colorful Quilts
Sew One and You're Done
Simple Gifts for Dog Lovers—*New!*
Simple Seasons
Skinny Quilts and Table Runners—
    New!
Spellbinding Quilts
Sudoku Quilts
Sweet and Simple Baby Quilts
Young at Heart Quilts
Your First Quilt Book (or it should be!)

Our books are available at bookstores and your favorite craft, fabric, and yarn retailers. If you don't see the title you're looking for, visit us at www.martingale-pub.com or contact us at:

1-800-426-3126

International: 1-425-483-3313
Fax: 1-425-486-7596
Email: info@martingale-pub.com